LOVELY ASUNDER

LOVELY ASUNDER

Poems by Danielle Cadena Deulen

The University of Arkansas Press
Fayetteville
2011

15   14   13   12   11   1   2   3   4   5

Designed by Liz Lester

⊗ The paper used in this publication meets the minimum requirements of the
American National Standard for Permanence of Paper for Printed Library
Materials Z39.48—84.

LIBRARY OF CONGRESS CATALOGING-IN-PUBLICATION DATA

Deulen, Danielle Cadena, 1979–
    Lovely asunder : poems / by Danielle Cadena Deulen.
        p.   cm.
    Includes bibliographical references.
    ISBN 978-1-55728-960-5 (pbk. : alk. paper)
    I. Title.
    PS3604.E84L68   2011
    811'.6—dc22
                                    2010049952

for Chris

ACKNOWLEDGMENTS

For their generous support of me and my work, I wish to thank Jay C. and Ruth Halls and the Wisconsin Institute for Creative Writing, the Rosenberg family, and all those at the Dorothy Sargent Rosenberg Memorial Fund, George Mason University's creative writing program, the University of Utah's creative writing program, and the Virginia Center for Creative Arts.

I am grateful to the editors of the following publications in which these poems appeared, sometimes in slightly different versions: *Missouri Review, Best New Poets 2009, Indiana Review, Southern Review, Hayden's Ferry Review, Crab Orchard Review, Locuspoint, Louisville Review, Cream City Review, West Branch,* and *Sou'wester.*

For their roles in bringing this project to fruition, a special thanks to Enid Shomer and all those at the University of Arkansas Press.

Thanks to my family for their love and support, especially my grandmother, Mary; my mother, Cecilia; my sisters, Mileah and Jasmine; my brother, Micah; and my cousin, Kari. For their guidance and encouragement in writing this book, I am immensely grateful to Jennifer Atkinson, Eric Pankey, Peter Klappert, Dana Levin, Louise Glück, Jacqueline Osherow, Kate Coles, Paisley Rekdal, Christopher Woodward, Shara Lessley, Alycia Tessean, Darcy Holtgrave, Dawn Lonsinger, Shira Dentz, Lindsay Bernal, K. A. Hays, J. Michael Martinez, Melissa Tuckey, Brian Brodeur, Kiley Cogis, Christian Teresi, Josh Baugher, Scott Weaver, Annie Noble, and Melanie McCabe.

Most of all, I am grateful to Chris Tanseer, to whom I have dedicated this book, for being supportive, being patient, and being in my life.

CONTENTS

Three

Lovely-asunder, Hopkins said of the hewn stars.

One

INTERROGATION

How did you get here in the wet garden
on your bloody knees, and where is
your mother's brown dress smelling
of nickels and butter? Why is your father
yelling from his bedroom window,
and what of the gun? Why can't you untangle
your ankles from the cucumber vines?
How does it feel to press your small, hot cheek
to their leaves? Can you hear the evening
sprinklers start up like gossip over the dry lawns?
Soon the whole world will be shining with lies—
doesn't that make it easier? Can you feel
the tall pines leaning away, closing the clouds
like white curtains? And the neighbors—
where is the old woman who always keeps
one yellow eye on her nectarine tree?
Why do you dream of finding the corpses?
Why do your father's eyes fill up with blackness,
and what of the gun? Why do you press
your hand to your chest when he aims?
Don't you know it won't keep him from shooting?
And where is your mother's brown dress?
Can't it hear you crying? Why won't it come home?
When his bullets pierce the tree instead of your body,
can you sense your face going suddenly calm
as the scent of the neighbor's lilac drifts toward
your pulse in the garden and hangs itself over your head

as if it had prayed for you all of its life and finally,
finally found you? How do you know, without the words
to say it, that you are the summation of a lifetime
of desire? And when you know, do the stars emerge
from blackness, or arrive like shots in the sky?

FOR MY SISTER IN THE RIVER

I am the voice of one crying in the wilderness.

—JOHN 1:23

I was trying to be cruel when I threw the rhododendrons in her hair.
It was spring and the petals were sticky, bruised and crimson
against her dark hair, but instead of crying she laughed, spun herself
into this photograph of a girl dancing in circles so fast her body blurs,
her head a deep magenta and earth. My sister is small and stronger
than she looks. In a decade she'll arrive late at the door, her lip split,
eye swollen shut, her baby girl blushed with tears (wound around her
like a delicate vine.) She'll walk into the kitchen, sit down on linoleum,
say *I'll never go back.* I'll want to believe I hear her voice filling with
her voice from the river we swam as girls, where we'd take turns being
John the Baptist, drenching each other in the muddy tide. Underwater,
I could feel my sister's skinny arms straining to pull me through currents,
lift me through the dark surface, press her fingers to my forehead, say
You're forgiven. You're healed. We were too powerless to be prophets.
I don't mean halos appeared above us in the river, or the kitchen was lit
by anything other than streetlight lost from the roads outside, just that
we knew, without psalm or song to guide us, we had to save each other.

FIG

The wolf that suckled Romulus and Remus rested
under a fig tree—a lignum known for its peculiar
inflorescence concealed within the body of its fruit.

Being neither fruit nor flower, but part of both, the fig
is really a hollow, fleshy receptacle enclosing a multitude
of flowers, which never see light yet come to full

perfection by ripening their seeds inward. Meditative,
already known as the Bodhi tree before Gautama
Buddha reached enlightenment beneath it. *Sing to me*

says my niece, my Preciosa, over the phone. Her small
voice drizzled in pear juice and honey, offered as a gift:
three round words on a white plate. Sweetness

is a sense we attribute to the innocent—naiveté,
a kind of protection from a light that might otherwise
ruin. And I would also keep her in a pod, if I could—

one of many flowers preserved in darkness. But then
an army invades Tibet. Women and girls are hung
from ceilings, beaten, starved, sterilized, and those

who are pregnant, forced to abort. I revise the song
and make her sing with me: *Watch for whomever the wolf*
suckles, Preciosa. The path through the orchard is dark.

CORRIDA DE TOROS

From earth, each star
is a likeness of the other, which is why divination
is impossible—the constellations are not Braille, but piercings,
wounds in the neck of a bull.

Perhaps the sky is a matador's scarlet.
Or, no—perhaps the sky is the stadium in which we sit, watching
the bull, the banderilleros stabbing his neck, the way he falters,
throws his head wildly, his yellow eyes trying to focus
on the source of pain—

The men drink from leather flasks of wine and the women
avert their eyes, or a few young men avert their eyes
and some young women lean toward the scene so far forward it seems
they'll fall out of the sky

toward the earth again, where their bodies will be trampled
or swell with children. The mothers fret at this,
their fingers drawing near the frayed ends of their daughters' hair
as if their children were fabrics they could weave
without touching. Everyone is yelling *Kill the bull,*

except those who murmur *I want to die*
into their palms, into the palms of their neighbors
who turn back to their wine, or stand and begin to weep.
The bull staggers and we swarm into the arena

to drive steel points trussed with ribbon
into his crest, his throat, his knees—until the matador
drops his sword, sprawls in the dust. Night shifts around us,
mud-dark and furious—clouds like white foam in the mouth
of the sky—and we stare a long while

at the scene we rendered, trying to recall
how we arrived. Slowly, the curved horn of the moon
rises. Lament settles in the stadium tiers.

Some in the crowd begin to chant *There is no balm
to assuage the mark of the body.*

Others sing *There is no star that leads us away from ourselves.*

IN A PAST LIFE, YOU WERE JOAN OF ARC

Little heroine, a dose
      of morale for the sad soldiers,

pick up the shine of your sword,
      but not the sword. You're hearing voices
again, early in the twenty-first century, that say

      Don't let the duke catch you
      talking to angels.

Or you're leaning from a tower
      in Rouen, in Manhattan, a swoon of sidewalk way
      down, feeling trapped
      by your own devices. It's 1430.

It's 2001. Spring—what are you doing
      with those boys in the field, in the dunes?
      They say they love you

now, but in a month when your body
is wounded, the only honor they'll give is
last in the field as they
retreat. No man wants to be led

      by a girl. Go back
      home. Make a bright northeastern bouquet

of lavender, willow branches, forget-me-nots. Soon
you'll be charged with passion
and heresy. *Don't let the duke catch*

>*your soft shoulders beneath*
>*that armor.* When you left,

it was winter. Your mother hid in the heather
> wringing her hands, and you took with you
just enough to stay hungry—

>a heel of bread, a cross, a canteen
>of plain water, the memory of your village
>burning.

How to Pray

Almond branches, wilting over the girl,
     look as if they are bowing,
          and the bend of her neck follows, or perhaps
(it might be too much to say) her neck bends

     and the branches follow. She's only a girl, after all,
          walking without permission beneath
a dangerously dim sky, in a grove large enough

     to lose a girl in—the roadside fruit stands
          shut up and emptied,
only a few cars heading home.

     It's 1964 in southern California
          and my mother's run away.

She's packed two pears, her new white dress,
     and a bible in the basket at the head of her bike,
          ridden until the lots stretched so vast they couldn't
be contained by borders, the sidewalks sprawling

     into gravel alongside the highway. She's gone
          looking for Canaan, or someplace closer to heaven

than Orange County, a dirt backyard enclosed
     by cyclone fences, her tanned brothers brooding
          on the back porch, their large, dark eyes

already done. She wants an angel to arrive—sleep
        without the dream of a distant house on fire across
            a narrow valley, smoke rising so quickly

it blackens the sky. She can't yet read
        the gathering clouds, the fever of consummation.
            In the almond orchard, her head bowed,
wilted blossoms scent her long, dark hair,
        her damp skin. My mother doesn't know how

            to pray for what she wants, only to imitate the wind
in her breath. Irrigation ditches draw long, dry sighs.
        The blooms threaten to catch fire. Between rows,
            dirt is mapped with tiny tributaries—not the lines

that lead to Canaan and its burdens—not water,
        but a promise of water, where water will run
            when it rains.

Allegory of Smoke and Music

He was a pianist, aging, no one famous. When there was still music, he played with famous people. He had long smokes with them between sets on days when the light yellowed a little, turned the smoke into veils. Now he taught. Between students, he smoked. After her lesson, one pale girl always followed him outside, no matter the weather, stood with him near the juniper and stone arches. She didn't smoke, had hair like spun honey, and he tried not to indulge her. The skin on the backs of her knees and the insides of her arms was so thin it seemed to him a sheet of music. She only spoke of her dream life. He spoke of nothing. At night, he dreamed of playing without touching the keys—the chords channeled through bone, nerve, the thin, blue wires of his veins. And when he couldn't sleep, he walked the mile to campus, to the red aisles of the concert hall, to the grand on stage, and lifted its chest, let silence quiver through the exposed strings—

Speak X

She taught me how to say *hello* and *goodbye* in Khmer—
sounds whose feel in my mouth I no longer remember,
like the broth she once poured over my tongue, something

of salt, spice, heat, or the incense she burned each night
before a small brass god whose many arms gestured toward
many exits, or points of arrival, the places I'd never been:

Here, she said, dropping her finger on a globe to a country
of blue and green, its hills warming beneath her hesitation
before *All the way to here*—sliding over mountains, oceans,

borders, to the classroom we shared for hours each day,
waiting for bells to release us. *In Cambodia, January
is a dry season,* she once said of our birthday month,

And in summer monsoons make floods. I imagined blue sky
soaking up green fields, the sun an orange fingerprint
blotted in the air, like the small, round scars on her belly

that she saw me see when we undressed for bed.
Cigarette burns, she said, once we turned out the lights
and our four arms rested beneath her thick blankets.

But I was small, my Mother says nothing to—but she finished
the sentence in Khmer, a language, and also a word meaning
"Speak X" and "I love you," depending on how your tongue hits

the consonants and where the vowels are placed: above,
below, in front of, after. In English, her last name was Oak,
spelled like the tree. Her first name: the memory of flight.

WRITTEN IN SKIN

XX are the initials of my first lover,
      the letters my sister tattooed
            into his shoulder with a single
needle and India ink. For two days

he sat on our wheat-colored couch wincing
      at the calligraphy he'd chosen. My sister's quiet
            eyes and quick hands, their precise
staccato, worked the ink into his skin

like a vow. She was prettier than I was and we all
      knew it. When he'd flinch, she'd press her small hand
            to his chest, say *Hold still,* and he would
hold still. She promised to scar me as well

when I decided on a design I'd want permanent
      in my skin, one I'd bleed for. But summer ended
            and our slender love withered. XX found a girl
as beautiful as my sister. I began speaking in crow,

withered branches, fields cut down for the harvest.
      My sister and I spun like moons through
            the rooms of the house until we forgot
how to speak entirely. Through winter.

Through a decade. And now that it's been too long.
      Now that my first lover is a boy whose name
            even he forgets, whose face is
a cloud, whose body has evaporated over the frozen

earth like the breaths of strangers. Now that I know everything
            permanent fades from the body. Now that the blank
                        skin on my shoulders. Now that the shape
of those years rises from the horizon. Now that my eyes.

Now that I know I can't take back what was
            never said. Now that the ink sinks into the shoulders
                        of the couch. Now that the ink well
is empty. Now that I've chosen. Now that the tip of

            the needle glints in my palm—

APOLOGIA

They were on a train, in a tunnel
between Brooklyn and Manhattan,
when he said he felt *quiet.* She asked
what quiet *felt like* and he said *small.*
She knew more about him then,
thought of how small he looked
the night she told him she was sorry
about their baby. The attic's slant
made everything smaller as she lay
with her ear to his stomach to listen
to him breathe. Music from a room
downstairs rose through the floor,
and when she told him, he went silent.
They listened to a solo, the steel-string
guitar holding and bending each long
note until it broke into the next.
When she realized he wouldn't speak,
she stood, left the house, and outside
everything was huge—the night, the trees,
the street became wider, longer as it led
to the park. She found two young men
beneath lamplight and oaks, unfolding
an American flag they said they stole
from a town near Mount Rushmore.
It was small at first, but unfolded and
unfolded until it veiled the entire field.
She thought of mundane expectation,
how a flag that size raised at the center

of a town might be seen for miles
in a South Dakota landscape—how
the people waking early, looking out
at the Black Hills in half light, must have
had a dim sense of something missing
as they sipped coffee, chewed, swallowed
their breakfast, stared out at the empty sky
the way we might in the first weeks of winter,
not quite seeing the bare limbs of trees,
not yet knowing why this sense of loss,
of displacement. And then her body felt
too small to hold her, so she left it—
drifted up through the pale lamplight,
the boughs of dark oaks, watched
one young man sprinting along the stripes,
the other shouting *the Pledge of Allegiance,*
and her body curled up over one giant star
like something unborn inside it.

I Want You Dangerously

open. But I am a woman, so cannot
      open you the way I would if (at the hinge
         of your spine, the tight latch

of your knees) I had a key, or hammer. I mean
      no violence, just as good men
         never mean violence,

but still I tremor, tremor. Your mouth
      a ruin—your eyes like the dark ascending
         wings of a bird—

I watch magpies destroy
      the nests of sparrows. Pillage.
         Plunder. If I were a Viking, I'd take you

home, my only and best prize.
      I'd marry you to my bones.
         Oh, tell me you want my

burnt sage, saltwater scent—my barricade
      across the roads of your body—or tell me
         to *leave you the fuck alone,* and I'll go

further inland, like a lenient
      hurricane—all of your beautiful
         levies intact.

ASUNDER

A woman turns to her white dress
frozen on the line. A man turns

nowhere, or toward an indeterminate space
near dried amaranth hanging
from garage rafters. Fixed angles.

Dried flowers. No one is saying
what they mean to say. The scene

smears off the canvas, interrupted
by a frame—offers no confession.
The artist prefers the story obscured, would never

place the two forms together or paint
their faces clearly enough for a crowd

to feel their expressions. She sees an absence
in the ruined dress. His eyes are closed.
He sees what we all see. I've lost

the explanation for the painting.
The guide has moved on to a discussion

of *the abstract*. When the crowd follows,
I'm left in the white echoes
of the halls, reminded of two dreams—

one in spring, in a gallery of ice, where portraits
hang bright on the melting walls.

The curator goes from frame to frame, each a more
distorted version of my face.
When I vie to tell her the doubles are lies,

my tongue swells with the ice.
Outside, I hear a northern thaw splitting

the landscape like gleaming teeth. I try to run,
but the dream leads to an August field
where I'm pressed down (in a white dress)

beneath a groom who tells me if I marry him,
I'll never again have to tell my story.

And when I say *I will,* he opens his fist, pours
a pile of ash at the center of my chest—says
If I married you, this is what they'd throw.

SUMMER WASPS

That was the summer I lay on my mattress
watching the wasps skim my window screen
the way they did the eyelashes of the girl
whose body we found beneath the overpass.

We were still children, thin and flat, and thought
nothing of how she'd arrived, only fascinated by
what she was then—blood cooled beneath her
skin, her dark hair, wind-knotted, face swelling

all those days we dared each other to walk past,
holding our breath, not knowing what the stink
meant. Finally, the rain-worn garbage bags,
a black cocoon that contained her body, split open.

When the policeman came, he taped off the site,
said we couldn't play there anymore and anyway
why would we want to, did we *know something
about this,* he said, *dead body,* and I discerned

a dead body: cars thrumming past, ants channeling
in skin, the indecipherable code of the wind—no
spirit loosed like a veil, no heaven opening to call her
home, her eyes blue as a sky that overlooks nothing.

The milky eyes of blindness. The gray stare of roads,
the roads I walked on so far away from there I could
never find my way back and by then I was a woman so
anyway why would I want to; I knew something about that.

TRUCE

I found you near an empty house, either
deteriorating or being built—too dark out
to see which. It was raining and you sat

on the sidewalk, legs splayed in a V, half sunk
in a muddy puddle, your eyes open but somewhere
else. You hadn't shaved for weeks and your beard

grew in red. You'd been crying too long
and were beyond it now, like one who drives
past his own house but doesn't have the heart

to circle back. You looked the way I felt
in the months after you left—bare oak limbs
mimicking a forest, a crow frozen on the lawn.

I reached down to you and your eyes filled.
You said you'd been sitting there regretting
the whole mess—you loved and still love me.

It was a dream, of course. *Forgive and forget,*
we like to say, as if forgivers go on forgetting
while the guilty tie themselves to the mast

of memory. I bent down and gathered you
up in my arms (your long body no heavier than
a loaf of bread), walked us through miles of dark,

looking for a single dry doorway to rest in, while
your soft mouth murmured against my shoulder,
I love you, you whore. You said it in your sleep.

FIRST WIFE

As I was leaving, he called me *Lilith*.
     His first act of erasure: my name
reduced to a lotus—a part
     he went to when he tired of coupling

with beasts. He wanted me
     to lie there beneath him—smother
in the smell of wool oil and sweat, his tongue
     a hard slug crawling over me. Yes,

I left. And when a woman leaves,
     she becomes a scandal. His sons said
I coupled with Satan—bore him
     a hundred new demons a day—

said I flew around at night, looking
     for newborns to strangle in their sleep.
The people hammered amulets above
     the beds of pregnant women

to warn me away. Still, mine was a slow
     attrition into apocrypha. After
they smoked my eyes, they sealed my dark hair
     in an urn. They buried the well of my throat,

left my nipples to dry, like figs in the dessert.
     The long columns of my legs were eroded
by rumor. Only my dark aria
     sang through. For centuries, celebrants

slept with one hand on their crotch, one hand
        on a crucifix—afraid I might conjure
a sweet dream. Finally, they took me
        out of the story. Perhaps you think

I'm exaggerating. But consider that poor, docile girl,
        pulled from Adam's own rib to replace me—
She tried to leave, too. You've heard
        what they say about her.

ANTARCTICA—

signifying a place opposite the *Arctic.*

A name of negation—as in, this place is called
not that place. This is the place

that is not a place, which must be why,
in dreams, this is where I die

and why I can't hear the glaciers crash
into ocean, feel the bitter wake

in the marrow of my sternum. *Why don't I
hear the wind? Why doesn't the wind split*

my exposed skin open? And my throat
so dry—ice drifts freezing against

my stone hips, the long horizon haunted
by light that won't rise—*I've arrived*

and this is where I die. Not *arktos,* but *antarktikos—*
not the Great Bear, but the bear

who opposed her. A fight named
by Aristotle, who never traveled so far,

or had reason to believe it might be true.
A fight that formed the earth—

two bears, the color of stars, rolling
in darkness—one head North,

the other South, revolving so slowly they forgot
their strife, gripped for the sake

of gripping, their growls becoming one deep,
continuous sound—a sound

we are born hearing, and so don't hear.

WHEN PANDORA OPENED HER BOX, SHE FOUND

an empty box. The moon, just a sharp hook of light above her—
lacuna in the flesh of the sky.

Sometimes the idea of the thing
is more dangerous than the thing itself.

And after, of course, the gods had someone to blame.

Two

PASTORAL

Isn't it terrible
the way the wind
goes on, a blind, breathing

field, traveling over us?
And isn't the constant light of the sun
demeaning, the way it burns

and burns but is never
consumed, while we are matches?
O, fiery seraph

guarding the darkness
alone, turn to me now
and tell me that this life isn't
a loosed gyre—

that when we were cast
out, with the sticky sweet of fruit
on our lips, a trail of bronze

pulp smeared across our bodies
where we had touched each other,
open-eyed, shaking beneath

palms, and shame, that bright
seed of knowledge, grew

in us until we knew we were
lost—tell me
you didn't mean forever.

Lost Letter I

I can see you here, your letter says, weeks before
it arrives. You are as timid as an unsliced
papaya beneath the soaked awning, rain barely
not wetting your thin, green shirt. *You could be
any one of these women walking past—each with
a dark umbrella over her face. You, where the rain
isn't.* I turn to answer, but your ship has left
for Korea, Vancouver, Chile. I have a lover,
and then I don't. Then I do again. This time
you call, but the blossoms of cherry trees
open in my mouth—sweet ghosts—tip of
your thumb on my sad lower lip. *Pittsburgh
is the city of a thousand bridges,* you said, the only
time we split together—the snow kept falling
over the windshield of your car, and I had no
reply. *When I have a daughter, I'll name her June,*
you told me, and I knew she wouldn't be mine.

LEMON

They loved each other, but a lemon tree
grew between them—no solace in the way
it leaned, as if to whisper from her yard

into his, across the coyote fence,
a promise of something greater. The fruit
was a luminous yellow, triumphant

in the branches—at night, he'd stare
at the tree's dim body, almost
indistinguishable from the darkness,

and imagine climbing into the V
of its trunk, swallowing the lemons whole,
his belly full of light. She'd quiver in

her bed, dream of her arms turning to wood,
snakes like ribbon over her radiant
throat, lemons ripe in her hair. They remained

hidden from one another, but gathered
the fallen fruit, rolled them on their bedroom
floors, severed them into halves—radial

as open compasses—ate the brassy
bitterness of their skins. Isn't this how
it would taste: a sour citrus sprinkled

with sugar, salt, the bitter aftertaste of rind?
Or do you place an apple in her hand,
a past sweetness in each crisp bite?

LOST LETTER II

We could rendezvous like children in a place
we build ourselves, make a roof from branches,
bittersweet and eyebright, choose whose body
will be the structural beams, whose body will be
the windows, doors. *If we are the house, who will
live in us?* No time for rational thoughts, my
Skeleton Key, just hold me in your arms like
a piñata broke open. *Why does this distance always
feel violent?* you said, but I heard *violet,* as in
lavender field, the under-rush of ocean. Connotations
abound, but nothing literal to hold. On the early
train home, I thought of the breaths you left at
the turnstiles, how I could have plucked them,
like plums, from the dark, morning air. My bones
felt light, almost hollow, and I'd have flown back
if you hadn't already relinquished our shy season
to the ice-paved roads, the trembling boughs.

PAPAYA

So far from home and her fever so high
it seems the swollen river at the edge of the city
speaks to itself, and the wild papayas hanging low

in the branches outside her window beg her
to slice them open so that she might plunge
her fingers into the pool of black seeds, leave

the sweet flesh bare in the light the way
her father did with the gutted trout, its silver
scales flaking off into the white ceramic sink,

belly cleaned of entrails and spawn—*This one
was pregnant,* he said, scooping the pink skein
into a jar he kept for bait. She thought

of her own body, the small clusters of eggs
inside her like tiny constellations, *like papaya fruit,*
her mother had explained to her that morning

in the kitchen, her father already gone to the river.
And when he returned, he took out his knife,
cut the fish from tail to throat, stuck his thumb

into its empty mouth and with one quick tug—
Her mother hummed in the other room,
stroking her round belly, waiting for the light

to open her. That night, her mother fried the fish
in cornmeal, salt—a slice of papaya on each plate.
She angered her mother when she refused to eat it.

Now, her eyes sting, though the air is humid, full
of stillness. The standing water outside her door whirs
with infection. She draws a thin curtain around her

so the air and mosquitoes can no longer touch her—
merely mottle the afternoon sun, insinuate their
forms like a gray swarm of ghosts over her body.

LOST LETTER III

You no longer remember my voice, so I call
on New Year's Day. *La Loteria* is stacked red
on your end table, beneath the unlit lamp.
Sharp light from the window reaches into your
eyes as you lift the receiver. You are surprised
to hear my voice out of nowhere. If you flipped
the top card over, you would find an umbrella,
then a moon, a cactus, a whale breaching the sea.
The Chinese symbol over your bed reads *poem*.
I want to tell you how I've been, but instead,
a lemon. Instead, a drum—its thick skin struck
over and over. Instead, a bell, a fiddle, a lobster,
a drunkard blurring through the frozen streets.
Instead, a horse, a train speeding terribly away.
If you believe this is our fate, then put our fate down
like a rabid dog, I try to say, but instead, the earth's
elliptical orbit, the lustrous plumage of crows.

POMEGRANATE

I say my sister ate
a pomegranate seed and already
you know the image before

the flame strikes
the darkness. You can see her
small, lean hands—a pale

glow in the caverns
of your mind, and the careful

dismantling of the white,
bitter body, a labyrinth
from which the garnet kernels
must be saved, eaten. And then,

what does that make
the seeds mean? In Hades
they would be planted in

a gold ring to keep her, but here
we are on a Tuesday in the twenty-first century,
and the myths we have lived by

are myths. We begin
with such vigor to know ourselves,
and then we get lost. She went
to find flowers on the plains of Enna.

The earth opened and my sister
was no longer my sister.

She became only
a story—a minor deity. See how
she fidgets in her underground
kitchen, how she stares up

and up into the dark, looking for exit.
The flame has burned down the wick

of her fingernail, and still burns.
Little candle. Little semibright ruin.
There she is with the pomegranate

heavy in her palm, starving
for the thing that will kill her.

Lost Letter IV

The lake in the landscape of our past was all
fog—we walked along it, our faces obscured,
our conversation cold-pressed, virgin olives.
I am a patient man you stated, and a buoy lit out
in the Arabian Sea. Listen, I couldn't hear you.
Anything I say about that afternoon, I have to
imagine—my tongue was underground, ruing
the taste of pomegranate. To be clear: the one
I left you for was a grave mistake. In spring,
even next to you, my heart was still damp. *Here,
eat some of these.* You handed me daffodils, bright
candy, little glints of light off the water. I'd lost
the word for kindness, felt ashamed. *I'm sorry.*
I'm sorry. Which one of us said it? I wanted to
hide my face in my sleeves, or for you to unclasp
my garnet necklace, slip the sad stone over my
bare torso, hush down the alleys of my thighs.

TOMATO

Go back to the garden—the green
scent of unripe tomatoes, a nightshade,
a cousin to belladonna, the extract
dropped into the eyes of courtly women to dilate
their beauty. You are too young

to know this. Still, your pupils widen
in the shade of the plant—the black dots of your eyes
unfurling like fists into palms.
You are calm, though
your father screams from somewhere behind you

from outside the garden, but he sounds so close
it's as if he rests his lips on the edge
of your earlobe. You are distracted
brushing the fine green hairs on the stem
of the tomato plant, breathing in its bitter scent.

You rub mud over your slack limbs
to hide, to become, again, unshaped, to stop
this moment from taking root in your mind,
to become a blind, burrowing thing. This is how
you learned to till the earth with the rake

of your fingers. This desire to inter yourself—
return to a seed, a small dot deep in
the flesh, to be inside the green, translucent fruit,

its thin skin, its seeds like distant stars, eyes
not yet burdened with opening. No.

No—opening is never a burden. You have only
seen what you wanted to see, heard
what you wanted to hear. What you fear
most is that your ruined garden isn't true,
that somewhere the wheat ascends, the delphinium

blooms, and you have walked through your life
eyes closed and so never saw it. Fear your own tongue's
bitterness. Fear your glut of sadness so deeply you rise
up from the valley—from the shadows of the garden—
open your eyes wide, hear your father singing.

LOST LETTER V

It's too late. Voices rising through the vents
awoke us from the dream we were having
of each other. I am a child and you snap off
an aloe leaf to soothe the scrape on my knee.
You are also a child and hide under the table
but can't articulate why. I want to give you
a reason, or a quiver of feathers or an apple,
because you look hungry. Earlier, we were late,
but now it's June and the rain assuages the sky.
Snowmelt rises into clouds. Here, take my rib
to form yourself. Here, take this ball of clay,
this kiln. Knead my body into a different shape.
Press it into your body. Throw us into the fire
just to see what happens next. Or, never mind.
Go back to sleep. Let the smoke of us drift
out of sight. It still gets dark so early. Soon
I'll put down my pen, burn this letter for light.

Plum

At the end of the platform a woman plays cello, the low notes
        echoing through the tiled station, and up the stained
cement stairs, out through the turnstiles, it is early February
        and plum blossoms open on their black limbs, ready

for something I am not. It's morning and already
        I imagine walking home in darkness, unlocking the door
while my landlady, who lives in the apartment below,
        watches, her eye on me from the threshold as I climb

the stairs. Go in. Stand there in the hallway—no one to speak to.
        I watch water tremble between rails of an approaching train.
This is a practice of longing. I want to hold it the way I hold
        returned letters, the citrus taste of skin, stars so deeply

imbedded in sky I can't see them. Lunar New Year,
        and plum blossoms carved into jade to signify resurrection.
On the lower east side, people sweep their houses of last year's
        bad luck. This is the shallow knowledge I bite down on

like the strip of wood issued to ancient Chinese soldiers, used
        for clenching between the teeth to ensure against speaking
in a surprise attack. The word for this is *xianmei*. But the translator,
        a native speaker of Chinese, misread the character as *mei,*

and against sense and warfare, took the meaning to be *hold a plum*
        in the mouth. Imagine the soldiers, linear and silent, climbing
the enemy's stone walls, only moonlight on their smooth foreheads,
        their black hair—each with a plum in his mouth. Imagine

the overripe fruit disintegrating into sweet granules, the tart skin
        slipping over your tongue as you try to taste it harder, wear it
through to nothing, because it reminds you of something you can't
        quite—distracted by the wall, the great thirst for spring gathering

at the back of your throat. You see how I've made you a soldier—
        myself, the sleeping enemy. Take pity on me—take the pit
from your mouth. Leave it on the threshold of my door,
        unspoken. Tomorrow, we'll have something to make sense of.

OVERRIPE

I'm tired of lust—the cut grass and cedar
scent of your skin, the way we arrive
to each other again and again—sick
of the brambles' blooming small, white
flowers, which will ripen

to heavy black, smother, rot
in dirt. What I loved of you
is plagued by wanting—desire
like a lesion in the mind. When you crush
against me, you leave autumn winds.

I am becoming cicada husk, the cool
throat of an empty vase, the dark space
between stars. You touch me and I see
that monstrous child Montaigne pitied
on the streets of Paris—my inseparable twin

hanging from the center of my chest,
your head where my heart should be, my heart
pushed aside. And if I am of two minds—
if I can't divide your body
from my body, but am still burdened

by the weight of you, then we can only
defeat each other. We are grotesque,
my love. The crowd pelts our bodies
with coins, and even the face of God
among them swears as he closes his eyes.

HEARTH

In every human heart, a ruined garden.
Blackberry thickets colonize my left
atrium—ripen in summer when God
makes a pie of me. *Delicious sinner.*

The oven is all in your mind, Buddha
recites, but I can't find a way to turn
the dial down. My dry skin splits and heals
in the swelter. Bodhisattva or not,

it hurts. *Cross my heart and hope to die,* I
swear, forgetting the rosary. Thorns,
in wanderlust, pierce the hard garden walls.

Lord, save me from the ordinary world.
A goldfinch flies into briars, gets stuck.
It quivers in there—little glint of light.

Three

LOVELY

My sister accuses me of leaving
        and staying gone. Her face has grown dim as she waits
        for a reason. Musk and winter darkness

cling to the heavy curtains hanging
        from her windows, crowding out
        the deep green of camellia leaves, their thin tips
                scratching her window, and beyond them

traffic blooming smoke in rain, thistle weed
        and wild grass growing in the busted
body of the pavement, no longer a smooth
gray bone the way it must have been
        when it was poured down a decade ago.

        I don't know, is all I can say. I know
        fog stands in the hills of the park down the street.

And on the other side of the park, a reservoir.
        And on the other side of the reservoir, an avenue
        of warm light and chatter, scones and fried pork,
rain beading up on the surface of umbrellas, buses,
        airplanes breaking through stratus to blue sky. Above

there are people nodding and smiling through
        compact windows, looking down at rain clouds,
        lightning, whole swaths of sky suddenly radiant

as pearls, as the meat of the apples we ate
in the summers of our childhood. *Translucents,*
they were called—tart and delicate,
ripe with light—

That was so long ago, sister. All forms, from a distance,
are lovely and bind us. We've tried to evade
the shapes others make of us—the sense of ourselves
built on those shapes. I was not the only one
to leave. Remember those boxes you kept
beneath your bed, tied with pretty red ribbon?

Remember the night you slipped out through
the window, barefoot down the slant of the roof,
dropped like dark fruit onto the streets alone,
left me to find your untied boxes,
each filled with the skeletons of birds?

APOLOGIA PRO VITA SUA

In Dorset, Millay and her mother walk together in the fields,
weaving between the timothy and wild geranium, like two ships
moving parallel on a bright green sea, each rivet a weed
they might pluck, eat. They want to resolve
her pregnancy—the poet and her nurse-mother, each
with a heart like a hull. One autumn, a friend of mine, a Catholic,
believing she was pregnant, stood each day at the aft of a ship
as it crossed the Atlantic from Boston to London. She let the wind
thrust against her body, fierce but invisible, like the spirit
of her lover's absence, until she could no longer feel it, until her body
was a net, passed through, and she no longer shook—her desperation

leaving behind a long wake. The mother gives her daughter dandelion,
mustard, pigweed, nettle. They walk for hours, ride horses,
eat rhubarb, but nothing, yet, makes her bleed. It's July 1922.
They are unaware of all crises except theirs. By then, Mahatma Gandhi
had rejected British rule and been tried for sedition.
The judge who sentenced him to six years in prison opened
his palms skyward when he said it to show how empty they were
of the decision, like the hands of my friend's lover,
loose on the steering wheel as he drove her to the pier
on the morning of her departure, tucked a stray
strand of her dark hair behind her ear, waved goodbye from the shore.
They'd talked it over and over—waves in an ocean of waves—

trying to imagine a room in which their tenderness
would not ruin them. In a cottage in the English countryside,
the daughter stares out of her bedroom window, her fingers

absently running over the bare grain of the sill, the sun
a pale glint in the glass. She squints, her eyes tired. In Italy,
Mussolini's Fascists run into fields and museums
stealing swords, muskets, single-shot rifles, table legs, garden hoes,
even dried fish as weapons against the king. Near Luxor,
in the Valley of the Kings, archaeologists dig
to excavate Tutankhamen from his royal sepulcher, thirty-three centuries
dead. In the kitchen, the mother works to unearth

the roots of Venus. She grinds herbs in a mortar, humming
a song she once sang to an ailing man, while her daughters
a hundred miles away, left alone in their spare, northeastern house,
lay themselves down to sleep. The man was dead by morning. She pauses
her grind, trying to remember his name. In August, a typhoon
will kill sixty thousand in China, and the mother will find among her notes
an herb called *alkanet*—hold her daughter's small hands
as the child passes out of her. She will never bear another.
Later, when my friend locks herself in a public toilet in London

and swoons as the fetus clots, rejects her, she'll think about
the way the wake seemed to pour endlessly away from her because
it was part of a design too large to conceive of—how the wake
becomes waves in an ocean of waves—how it was only her small,
persistent concern that made it significant. When the mother dies,
the daughter will honor her wish to be buried beneath cherry trees,
though the land is pure rock, and she'll have to blast the earth open
to give her mother back. Cherry blossoms still fall over the quarry
of her grave—drift over fields and mudstone ocean cliffs, into the air
where they burn in the heat of passing planes, fall to the earth as ash.

Lotus Eater's Wife

I understand why you might
        prefer it to remembering,
love. In the dusk you embarked,

the water turned away,
        and I could almost see the slow,
constant rocking of the ship,

the hard winds and western
        loneliness deepening the salt
in your heart. In your memory now,

there is no wake—no seagulls
        circling the slack, half-massed sails,
no lime-water fetid in barrels,

no woman crying, no woman crying
        a ballad from the cliffs
you couldn't find through a fog,

from a poorly drawn map.
        And it must be so easy for you now,
eating and drinking, and butchering

cattle by the shore, the sometimes
        flashes of faces you can no longer
name emerging and ebbing and ebbing

until everything erodes into sand, sky,
        water—I wonder which tide pools
your fractured memory lingers in.

Which pieces are you surprised
        to find, to roll around in your
large palms? Which sighs do you keep

in your sad, heavy pockets?
        Which do you throw back to sea?

CIVILIAN SONNET

A cyclone fence divided an open field
from an open field. The runway bloomed with heat.
We smoked inside your car, the vinyl seats
sweating beneath our thighs. Your broken windshield
fragmented the sky. You turned to me, as if
to sing an aria, but your voice was lost
in roar and bray—an engine's jet exhaust
propelling the plane above us. Meteors drifted
like dandelion seed in the cold black
I wished was heaven. This was before the war
went on without you. Now the wind abrades
the dunes, then stills—your face, a flag gone slack.
Night falls. I close your picture in a drawer.
I know I should feel sad, but I'm afraid.

MORRO DE SÃO PAULO

Saltwater and hibiscus guide me toward waking
and I wake.

The last image of the dream comes back to me—
Caravaggio's *Conversione di San Paolo*

hanging on the air above the sea.

The image is so strong I have to remember where I am—
an island off the mainland of Brazil. Not home.

Not the cool-river north, cedar scent of home. I've slept
too long—a meridian sunset burns through my window.

Across the wooden floor, a canvas of sand.

I wish I had that painting in my hands—that bright saint
in a fit in the dust, the huge, looming horse,

its long neck bent over Paul as he flails
in ecstasy beneath a raised hoof.

The old groomsman in the corner bows toward

the horse, grasping the bridle in his one lit hand.
In peripheral darkness, he faces the ground. How strange

that he doesn't see what Paul sees. I sip a glass of dark
sugar rum, listening to the voices

I no longer recognize churn like waves on the shore.

——

The village contains a single road which I walk along
seared by the light of restaurant patios—

a pale amber glow over each patron's face, each mouth
an unstitched seam. The ocean sighs and sighs and sighs.

Always a samba plays furiously somewhere.

During daylight the island slept, but now it's crowded,
loud. A group of men yell a toast in Portuguese,

crash their caipirinhas. Long-limbed women with toasted skin
stand along storefronts, their stilettos sinking

like roots into sand. Each wears hibiscus behind her ear.

Their faces are lovely, but their eyes are hard—filled with loss—
sand and sky and loss—sand and samba

and the sound of ice clinking in rum. A man waves a bill
beneath a woman's face. She kisses him as she crushes

the bill between her breasts, turns away.

I pass the same scene again and again with slight
variations of plot, slightly different faces. Maybe

the woman demands more for the kiss. Maybe the crowd of men
becomes a crowd of young women.

Between houses there are trees with mangos heavy as moons,

and beneath the trees there are lovers. At least,
I call them lovers. I don't know what they call themselves.

————

Now the village is a loose rope of lights along
an indefinite shoreline—

Past the border, a sea I know only by sound
and the salt mist it exhales on my skin.

Beyond the sea there is nothing. In darkness at the edges

of the canvas an old groomsman stares at the dirt,
tries to settle the startled horse as the radiant,

fractured, epileptic saint flings his arms toward the sky.

He was blind for three days before Ananias touched his eyes—
And like as he possessed heaven, so he despised all earthly things;

and like as iron that is laid in the fire is made all fire—
I wonder if his bones, deep in the earth,

would blaze if I touched his painted face.

At the pier, I take the path that leads up a cliff.
The jungle thickens to my left, and to my right

a long drop down. As I climb, my view of the ocean
widens—becomes less intimate, more lucid.

The road plateaus at an empty church, its doors

open, and along the pews and sills are candles
flickering for no one. At the altar, a sermon of wind.

————

Forget the painting. Let's start, instead, with the vision.
Begin with the flash of light—

No, begin with the road opening and his face turning hot—
electric aura gathering in the temporal lobe.

His stomach deepens in his body and he senses

he's seen all of this before, as if the steps of the horse
go before the steps of the horse—stars suddenly

filling his mouth—heat and voice in a glittering
thunder reaching his ears before he could hear it.

He sees his body falling before it falls,

forgiven before he can ask forgiveness. I don't suffer
the saint's affliction—the affliction of light.

I walk in the upper canvas, staring at the ground,
afraid of men so overthrown by their own minds

as to believe they hear the voice of God.

I don't pretend to understand the prescience that comes,
or the blindness that follows. I keep to the road,

which wavers, disappears, reappears. Obscure in the far
dark corners of the island—restaurants closed, the last ship

gone for the mainland—I bend my body forward

like the branch of that first and most dangerous fruit.
When I turn back, the low glow of forgotten fires

riles the dunes where hushed voices rise
as an ache of wind bending through sea grass—

the peculiar call of lost birds.

THE DIVINERS

They need water, so they tell the simple girl
to snap a forked branch from the apple tree,
hold it gently in her dirty, upturned palm
so that the Y of the shape stretches out before her,
parallel to the horizon. *Walk slowly,* they say,

Close your eyes. But an apple is a pome,
a false fruit. The branches fork only
to confuse, like the apples themselves,
each seed refusing the likeness of its parent—
an act of survival. There is no pattern

to show her the way. When she arrives, if
water is below, the rod will turn in her hand,
bend toward the earth like a magnetized needle.
All day, this doesn't happen. Salt gathers
at the corners of their mouths—crops fading,

fated for drought. And now the light
is hungry, wild for darkness. They want to divine
a way to the water, but the branch is weary.
The girl is sullen. She drops the Y to hold
her face in her hands. Everyone rushes to dig.

SANGRIA

She lifts the bottle to her chest and pours
as if the wine had been waiting in her heart,
denying itself the memory of air, the taste
of a cool, thin glass, a lower lip, a tongue stained
red with its longing for a kiss of raspberry and smoke.
She slices oranges, lemons, nectarines. She opens

their round bodies, their sun-colored skins. She opens
the windows, lets the scent of anise and marigold pour
in from the garden. A distant fire, full of juniper smoke,
warns in the hills, channeled like blood from a heart
to the tips of fingers—a charred touch staining
the landscape black. What she wants is a taste

of flame, but sips a spoonful of sugar and wine to taste
what is missing—champagne, ice, a letter opened
alone each day at noon, the words stained
into paper with creases like canyons—years pouring
over the bluffs into silence, into the heart
of this room, where a woman sits at a table to smoke.

The table, like her hair, her eyes, is the color of smoke.
She tears the letter, places a piece on her tongue to taste
its bitterness—more bitter than glaciers, their heartless
bodies shrinking and swelling untouched. She opens
a drawer in the table, finds her deck of cards and pours
the suits from one hand to the other, letting her fingers stain

the edges with wine, while outside a burning horizon stains
the dry fig orchards and air with wine-colored smoke.
She thinks of a game her mother taught her. She pours
herself a drink from the pitcher. The soaked fruit tastes
like dusk—she swallows with her lips slightly open.
The players' aim was either to avoid the hearts

completely, at every turn and glance, or win all hearts.
She places the cards, the letter, her hands on the table, its stain
worn down to a splintered surface. She finds the queen, opens
the letter, drowns them in sangria. Her lungs, full of smoke,
constrict and shudder like a butterfly. The air tastes
of summer constellations that have no more light to pour

down. She rises to open the window further, let in
the smoke. Fire pours into the house. The soaked letter stains
the wine. No need to taste it again. She knows it by heart.

ALLEGORY OF THE WINTER DOE

A young man, walking alone at night because his car broke down, came across a doe frozen along the highway. Snow fell lightly on her pelt, her opened eye. Black blood iced a small space in the ditch. He crouched down to touch her neck. He had tasted venison the summer before, at a dinner where the woman he loved kept glancing at the friend who had shot the deer, skinned it, sizzled its meat on his grill. It made him feel sick to eat it and the sickness carried him out of the yard, down the road, along the curve of streetlights glowing over the rough, tangled limbs of pines. As he walked, he thought of the nights he lay awake while she slept. How the moonlight glazed her eyelids blue. How her chest rose so slightly, it seemed she hardly breathed. That must be why I awoke some nights, his hands slipping away from my throat—why I always slept in fits—dreamed of nothing.

Stein in Love with Picasso

          wanted to gather him like stars.
The calligraphy of stars, and oh how his eyes

are the black space between them.
Crucibles, really.
                    Things changed there. And his tightly
       wound body:
the intricate musculature of his wrists,

the way he twisted color, form. To be his object
was the object.

How his jaw flexed as he chewed. How many oceans
he could pour down his throat.

      His appetite. The way he could pick
      women like fistfuls of flowers, forget them
               on his table, or let them wilt
        in the street—how thirsty they were.

                And what beauty they had.

And how much they didn't matter. Only she
perceived. Only she was the map
he was guided by.

          If her body were a canvas.

After she sat for him, let him erase
and reshape her face,

she asked Alice one night to take
the paintbrush between her teeth and all over her body—
But Alice was no artist.

      Picasso, Picasso with his brute chest
          exposed to the sun—painting in the waves—

    pigment in the waves. The stray
    brush-stroked ochre ocean and pink bodies
    mangled—how he created

the world she saw, all the eyes
fractured—the sun shining like a red mirror. And in his absence

     she dreamed of Spain—a blood orange over
the Sunday roofs of Barcelona, night quivering
     like an archer's unsteady arrow,
       like the low throng

of cathedral bells, hours silenced. A woman singing
from a distant window in the long,
sad lines of Arabic—a prayer

like a current. Knife
on a table, light and dull. Wheat swaying
     beneath stars. Loosed
      oxen wandering, bewildered

in a dark lemon grove, pulling
     the weight of her heart.

Notes on the Passion Flower

Corona in the Crown of Thorns. Bright
stigmatic blossom. Aromatic fruit.
The mild, succulent pulp bears a slight

resemblance to clouds. Bitter, toxic root.
Narcotic used for sleepless souls, hysterics,
and those in love—drink fast and don't dilute.

Serrated leaves. The vine, a kind of helix
that thrives in torment—sweet green scent of lies.
The open blooms set fire to hearts like wicks.

Volcanic temperament provokes your eyes.
Your wrists a delicate cage. Scarlet tongue.
The bud confesses what the seed denies.

Each dusk your potent light unloosed has wrung
my mind like a rag. I curse these unnamed lands.
Nights like a sieve. Days like a song unsung.

I've traveled far. The road and sky expands
what's lost between us. Still, I can't unweave
our tangled vows. My prayers, my arrogant plans,

and all these thirsty years a dark reprieve
from you, my *Passiflora incarnata*.
If you told me you were holy, I'd believe.

In a Past Life, You Were Judas Iscariot

The bright musk of neroli follows you
     everywhere, a sweet guilt for something

     you can't remember you've done. Shiver
     of insects in the grove—

sanguine, earth-shaped fruit, heavy
on the branch and oh what gloss
those branches have. You calculate

     the density of silver, the way moonlight
         settles on the leaves. The leaves broaden out

     into spades, hearts, whatever seduction takes
     the shape of in your mind. Out on the tarmac

propellers hum, slice through the rain.
Your mouth is full of spring, white florals,
spice. *I will betray you,* you repeat

     though you don't know why. You are dizzy, shine
         with oil, want to kiss a stranger, or run out

     to the runway, drop down before the blank
     face of the plane, hang a rope from its great metal

arms, outstretched, let it raise you over the airport,
the hushed orchards of your mind, the city streets
lined with light. You believe this will save you—

the scent of your own unlit body swaying in the air,
      the surrender of each round light like an eye

on a bough of eyes, dropping farther,
deeper toward the pitch-dark earth.

PRODIGAL DAUGHTER

I return with a dime of light in my throat.

I return with empty pockets and a wild-eyed stallion.

I return with the bones of a whale—our names
carved in Sanskrit along the curves.

I return with quince seeds and promise an orchard.

I return when it is raining lightly in the afternoon
and you are sighing toward the window for nothing.

I return with sunburned feet and wheat in my hair.

I return with a winter mudslide.

I return while you are dreaming of your house
which looks nothing like your house.

I return with an artichoke, three acrobats, and clove
cigarettes.

I return with scrolls of papyrus and the boulder I am chained to.

I return with a drowned body on an unlit pyre.

I return when our father has died of complications.

I return with an iron kettle filled with gardenia perfume.

I return with an answer to all existential dilemmas.

I return with a fortune cookie that has misspelled *fortunate*.

I return for your marriage beneath live oaks, hands over
hands, the sky a kind of champagne.

I return alone.

I return with the letters I didn't send and a bottle of Oaxacan sand.

I return with your blessing, or I never return.

I never return.

FOR YOU

I once read a poem that compared
a pomegranate to a heart. And there
were sparrows darting in and out
of the lines, violets throwing off
the moonlight like an old coat,
and a student raising her hand to say
I don't get it. Someone loved someone
else, though someone else didn't love
someone back, or someone else did
but there was an obstacle. Maybe
the sparrows darted dangerously
near the pomegranate and pierced it,
or the violets stole someone's letters,
kept them folded in their small blossoms
because they believed they deserved them
more than someone else. This poem
is based on that one. And also on
the time we took a scenic route through
aspens and you told me how they always
spread after a fire season because
when the pines burn down they leave
enough space for new trees to grow.
The poem was entitled, "For You."
And we kept driving and driving until
winter came, smoothing the roads white
with tiny combs of ice—your fingers
ready to sculpt my shape out of snow

so that you could ease into the hollow
chest and leave a pomegranate safe
from sparrows—the violets suddenly
confessing everything to the student
whose face opens like sunrise when
she says *I understand now. I understand*—

NOTES

Fig

According to the myth, Rome was erected in the place where Romulus killed his twin brother, Remus. This poem is a collage with text taken from *A Modern Herbal,* by Mrs. M. Grieve (Harcourt, Brace & Company, 1931).

Corrida de Toros

The figure of the bull in Spanish bull fighting is considered a symbol of the martyrdom of Christ.

Apologia Pro Vita Sua

In 1922, when Edna St. Vincent Millay became pregnant by a man she did not intend to marry, she and her mother, Cora, fled to Dorset, England. Cora, skilled in nursing, fed Edna herbal concoctions that brought about Edna's miscarriage.

Morro de São Paulo

Suggested by Caravaggio's *Conversione di San Paolo,* which depicts St. Paul's conversion on the way to Damascus.

The Diviners

Suggested by Jim Leonard Jr.'s play *The Diviners.*

Stein in Love with Picasso

Suggested by Stein's obsessive literary portraits of Picasso.